THE LITTLE DOG
That Couldn't Match
THE FURNITURE

by Jean Corona

The Little Dog dreamed every day
of having his own home. It really didn't
matter what it looked like;

Just as long as he had a loving human
to take care of him, Just the way
he would take care of them.

But, it was more difficult than
he thought, Because it seemed like,
no matter how hard he tried...

He couldn't fit in.

Home

He realized –
that to be a good match for
his new owner,

He would have to make himself blend in.
But his first attempt didn't work.

The furniture and décor of the house
just didn't look like him at all.

It was bright and full of reds and
purples, and he was just – too brown.

And, before he knew it...

...He was alone again.

The next time he was adopted –
he was prepared.

He decided to try very hard
to be like the people
he would be living with,

Even if it meant looking really silly.

But maybe,
he tried too hard,
he thought,

Because before he knew it...

Home

...He was alone again.

Well, I can't be all that uninteresting,
he thought;
at least they take me home;
they just don't keep me.

So, he gathered his strength and
looked forward to the next adoption.

He just knew he could fit in this time.

And he would do anything, he thought,
to be a good match for someone.

But, even bending over backwards
and forwards, and
standing on his head, didn't work.

...He found he was alone again.

So, he thought,
maybe I just need to be
more sophisticated and cool.

So, this time, he tried very hard to
fit in by being very worldly.

But, the people who owned the
house could see right through
his masquerade.

And before he knew it...

Home

... He was alone again.

By now, his sadness filled the cage.
His tears of loneliness created
a long trail of tears from
the door of the dog store...

...out to the main street, past the
stores downtown and right into
the yard of a very nice little girl!

She was playing outside,
and looked down to find
pools of water all around her.

She knew that someone
was very lonely and needed love.

So, step by step she began to
follow the trail of tears…

He had been crying so hard
his eyes were swollen shut...

...then, he heard someone
tapping on his cage.

He didn't want to see
who was there because he was
so tired of being disappointed.

Finally, he opened one eye.
And that's when he saw her.

A little girl, holding money in her
little hand and pointing at him.

He was so excited when he saw her.

But he was afraid because
he knew that his efforts to be loved
in the past didn't work.

So, he decided, this time,
he would just be himself.

And, to his surprise, he found that he was, and probably always had been, <u>the perfect match.</u>

THE END

For all the dogs and cats
still looking for a forever home.